Wr

Poc

CW00376766

OCR Gateway A
Chemistry 4, 5 and 6

For GCSE Chemistry
Higher Tier

For all the science teachers I have worked with over the years...and for those I will work with in the future.

Subscribe to Wright Science on YouTube to for a full set of videos to support you in your GCSE science studies.

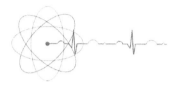

WRIGHT SCIENCE

SCIENCE DONE THE WRIGHT WAY

ISBN-13: 9781092627702

C4
Predicting and Identifying Reactions and Products

C4.1.1: Group 1 - The Alkali Metals

The group 1 metals are very reactive with oxygen and water so they are stored in oil to prevent them reacting with the oxygen and water in the air.

They show typical properties of metals:
- Shiny when freshly cut
- Conduct electricity
- Solid at room temperature

They demonstrate the following trends as you go down the group:
- Get softer (easier to cut)
- Density increases
- Melting point decreases

All group 1 elements have 1 electron in their outer shell so they all react in a similar way.

The reaction with water can be summarised as:

Metal	Observation
Lithium	Fizzed slowly
Sodium	Turned into a molten ball; moved quickly and fizzed quite a lot
Potassium	Caught fire and burns with a lilac flame; moves quickly; fizzes lots; can explode

General Word Equation:
Metal + Water → Metal Hydroxide + Hydrogen
Change the "metal" for the name of the metal.

General Balanced Symbol Equation:
$2M (s) + 2H_2O (l) → 2MOH (aq) + H_2 (g)$
Change the "M" for the symbol of the metal

E.g. For the reaction of sodium and water:

Word equation:
Sodium + Water → Sodium Hydroxide + Hydrogen

Symbol equation:
$2Na$ (s) + $2H_2O$ (l) → $2NaOH$ (aq) + H_2 (g)

> Exam hint: If you hate balancing – Just remember to put a 2 in front of everything except the hydrogen.

The reactivity increases as you go down group 1 because it becomes easier to lose the outer shell electron. This is due to there being more electron shells meaning the outer shell is further from the nucleus so the force of attraction holding the outer shell electron is weaker.

C4.1.2: Group 7 – The Halogens

Group 7 occur as diatomic molecules (pairs of atoms). E.g. Cl_2

> *Exam hint: You must remember that all halogens are diatomic or all balanced equations with them will be wrong!*

The halogens have typical properties of non-metals such as being brittle and poor conductors of electricity.

Halogen	State at room temp.	Colour
Fluorine	Gas	Pale yellow
Chlorine	Gas	Green
Bromine	Liquid	Orange
Iodine	Solid	Grey
Astatine	Solid	Dark grey/black

They demonstrate the following trends as you go down the group:

- Gas → Liquid → Solid
- Melting and boiling points increase
- Get darker in colour
- Density increases

Exam hint: If asked to work out missing values for boiling point or melting point, work out the differences between the given values and use that to give a more accurate estimate.

They react with metals to produce salts.

General Word Equation:
Metal + Halogen → Metal Hali**de**
Change "Halogen" for the name as it is on the periodic table (ends -ine). Change "Halide" for the halogen name but change the ending to -ide.

General Balanced Symbol Equation:
$$2M + X_2 \rightarrow 2MX$$
Change "M" for the symbol for the metal.
Change "X" for the symbol for the halogen.

E.g. Sodium + Chlor**ine** → Sodium Chlor**ide**
$$2Na\ (l) + Cl_2\ (g) \rightarrow 2NaCl\ (s)$$

The halogens all have 7 electrons in their outer shell so they all have similar chemical properties. They will gain one electron to make an ion with a single negative charge:
$$X_2 + 2e^- \rightarrow 2X^-$$

Their reactivity decreases as you go further down the group as it is harder for the element to gain an electron as the outer shell is further from the nucleus, so the force of attraction is weaker.

C4.1.3: Halogen Displacement Reactions

Halide: Compound of a halogen and one other element (usually a metal or hydrogen).

In a displacement reaction, a more reactive halogen will displace a less reactive halogen from the halide.

To carry out halogen displacement reactions:
1. Place 3 drops of the first salt solution into a well on the spotting tile.
2. Add 3 drops of the first halogen.
3. Look for a colour change.
4. Repeat with the other halogens and salts.

The results of a halogen displacement experiment would look like this:

	NaCl	NaBr	NaI
Cl_2	X	✓	✓
Br_2	X	X	✓
I_2	X	X	X

Half equations can be used to model what happens to each reactant.

$Cl_2 + 2e^- \rightarrow 2Cl^-$ (Reduction as electrons are gained)

$2Br^- \rightarrow Br_2 + 2e^-$ (Oxidation as electrons are lost)

The ionic equation combines the two half equations to make:

$Cl_2 + 2Br^- \rightarrow 2Cl^- + Br_2$ (Redox as both oxidation and reduction have taken place.)

C4.1.4: Group 0 – The Noble Gases

Group 0 are called the noble gases as they are unreactive and do not take part in many reactions.

Key properties:
- All non-metals
- All gases at room temperature
- Have full outer shells and so are not reactive

The noble gases are monatomic which means they are single atoms with weak forces of attraction between them.

They are gases at room temperature as the boiling points are low due to the weak forces of attraction between the atoms being overcome easily with limited amounts of energy needed.

Trends as you go down group 0 are as follows:

- Attractive forces between the atoms gets stronger as the atoms get larger
- Boiling point increases due to increased forces of attraction
- Density increases

C4.1.5: The Transition Metals

The transition metals are found between group 2 and group 3 on the periodic table.

They are all metals and show typical metal properties:
- Shiny when freshly cut
- Good conductors of electricity
- Strong
- Malleable

When compared to group 1 metals, the transition metals:
- Are stronger
- Are harder
- Have a higher density
- Have a higher melting point
- Produce coloured ionic compounds whereas group 1 produce white or colourless compounds.

The transition metals will react very slowly, if at all.

Metals like platinum and gold do not react with water or oxygen.

Iron will react with water and oxygen to make hydrated iron (III) oxide or rust.

The transition metals can form more than one type of ion. The Roman numeral in brackets tells us the charge on the metal ion.
E.g. Iron (III) oxide has Fe^{3+} ions.

The transition metals are good catalysts. This means they speed up chemical reactions without being used up themselves.

C4.1.6: Reactivity of Elements

Metal Reaction

Metals form positive ions. The more easily this happens, the more reactive a metal is.

A metal can react with water or acids if it is more reactive than hydrogen.

Metal + Water → Metal Hydroxide + Hydrogen

Metal + Acid → Salt + Hydrogen

In reactions where a gas is made, the volume of gas produced in a certain time can be used to determine the rate of the reaction. The more gas made, the faster the rate.

Measuring gas in an experiment can be done by:

- Counting bubbles. The volume of bubbles will vary and increases chance of human error in counting.
- Filling a measuring cylinder with water and inverting it in a tub of water. Place a delivery tube from the reaction vessel to under the measuring cylinder to collect the gas. Some gas may be lost if the tube slips from under the measuring cylinder.
- Connect a gas syringe – Most accurate

Displacement Reactions

In a displacement reaction, a more reactive metal will displace the less reactive metal from solutions of its compounds.

These reactions are redox reactions as both a reduction and an oxidation reaction take place.

Useful Patterns from the Periodic Table

- Group 0: Do not react
- Group 1 and 2 become more reactive as you go down the group.
- Group 7 become less as you go down the group.
- Group 1 and 2 are more reactive than the transition metals and other metals
- Metals may form ionic compounds with reactive non-metals.
- Reactive non-metals may form covalent compounds with each other.

Check Your Understanding

1. Explain the pattern in reactivity as you go down group 1.

2. What is the balanced symbol equation for potassium reacting with water?

3. Explain the pattern in reactivity as you go down group 7.

4. Explain what happens when you mix chlorine water with potassium iodide.

5. Why are group 0 known as the noble gases?

6. Explain what is meant by the term catalyst.

C4.2.1: Detecting Gases

To test for carbon dioxide:
Limewater goes from colourless to cloudy.

Limewater is calcium hydroxide solution.
When calcium hydroxide reacts with
carbon dioxide, water and calcium
carbonate (white precipitate) is made.

To test for chlorine:
Damp blue litmus paper turns red then
white.

Chlorine is an acidic substance so it turns
the litmus paper red. Then it bleaches it
making it white.

To test for hydrogen:
A lit splint makes a squeaky pop sound.

To test for oxygen:
A glowing splint relights.

21

Safety for detecting gases:
- Never inhale directly from the container!
- Hold the container a few centimetres away and gently waft the smell towards you and take a cautious sniff.

C4.2.2a: Detecting Cations - Flame Test

As metals burn or explode, the metal ions are vaporised. They absorb energy and the electrons jump to higher electron shells. As the electrons drop back to their normal electron shell, light energy is transferred to the surroundings as radiation.

Different metal ions can be identified by the colours they produce in a flame test.

To carry out a flame test:
1. Clean the nichrome wire loop in concentrated hydrochloric acid and holding it in the flame. Repeat until the flame does not change colour.
2. Dip the loop into the test powder/solution.
3. Hold in a roaring flame and note the colour.

Metal	Ion	Flame Test Colour
Lithium	Li^+	Red
Sodium	Na^+	Yellow
Potassium	K^+	Lilac
Calcium	Ca^{2+}	Orange-red
Copper	Cu^{2+}	Green-blue

Exam hint: You need to remember these colours and the ions they identify.

A common source of error is contamination from another chemical.

C4.2.2b: Detecting Cations – Hydroxide Precipitate Test

Group 1 hydroxides are soluble in water whereas most other metal hydroxides are insoluble in water. This is why we use sodium hydroxide in experiments.

When sodium hydroxide is added to a solution containing metal ions, a precipitate is formed. The colour depends upon the metal ion present.

Metal	Ion	Hydroxide Precipitate Colour
Iron (II)	Fe^{2+}	Green
Iron (III)	Fe^{3+}	Orange-brown
Copper (II)	Cu^{2+}	Blue
Calcium	Ca^{2+}	White
Zinc	Zn^{2+}	White

Exam hint: You need to remember these colours and the ions they identify.

To differentiate between zinc hydroxide and calcium hydroxide, you add an excess of sodium hydroxide solution. The zinc hydroxide will dissolve whereas calcium hydroxide will not.

C4.2.3: Detecting Anions

Anion = Negative ion (Attracted to the anode)

Cation = Positive ion (Attracted to the cathode)

Testing for Sulphate Ions, SO_4^{2-}

- Add a few drops of dilute hydrochloric acid (removes any carbonate ions present).
- Add a few drops of barium chloride, $BaCl_2$.
- If a white precipitate forms, sulphate ions are present.

$$Ca^{2+} (aq) + SO_4^{2-} (aq) \rightarrow BaSO_4 (s)$$

Testing for Carbonate Ions, CO_3^{2-}

- Add a few drops of hydrochloric acid.
- If bubbles of gas are made, carbonate ions are present.

$$2H^+ (aq) + CO_3^{2-} (aq) \rightarrow CO_2 (g) + H_2O (l)$$

Testing for Halide Ions

- Add a few drops of dilute nitric acid (removes other ions present to avoid a confusing precipitate)
- Add a few drops of silver nitrate solution, $AgNO_3$ (aq).

The colour of the precipitate tells you which halide ion is present:
- White = Chloride
- Cream = Bromide
- Yellow = Iodide

C4.2.4: Instrumental Methods of Analysis

Instrumental methods of analysis rely on machines to carry out the analysis on a substance.

Advantages:
- High degree of accuracy
- Very fast and can run 24/7
- Very sensitive and can analyse small amounts of samples (useful if expensive or difficult to obtain)

Gas Chromatography

A gas chromatogram is a chart that represents the different substances in a mixture.

Each peak is a different substance as the retention time is different for each substance.

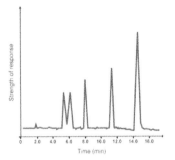

Areas under the peak show the relative amount of the substance.

Retention time is the time taken for a substance to travel through the chromatography column.

<u>Mass Spectrometry</u>

Mass spectrometers measure the masses of atoms and molecules.
They are used to analyse the relative amounts of isotopes and the structure of molecules.

When a sample enters the mass spectrometer, the sample is ionised to form molecular ions.   As these molecular ions gain energy, they may fragment. As these ions then pass through the machine, the detector records the amount of each fragment.

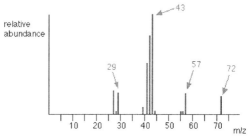

In a mass spectrum:
- The peak on the far right is the molecular ion. This is the relative formula mass of the molecules.
- Each peak represents a fragment of the molecule.
- Height of the peak tells you the relative amount.

Infrared Spectrum

The infrared spectrum shows peaks for the wavenumbers present within the chemical. This tells us what types of bond are present in the molecule.

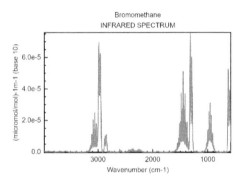

Check Your Understanding

1. Explain how to test for carbon dioxide.

2. Explain the gas test for hydrogen.

3. Explain the gas test for chlorine.

4. Explain the gas test for oxygen.

5. Explain how to use flame tests to identify an unknown chemical.

6. Explain how to use hydroxide precipitate tests to identify an unknown chemical.

7. Explain how to identify the anion present in an unknown chemical.

8. Describe the advantages of using instrumental methods of analysis.

C5
Monitoring and Controlling Chemical Reactions

C5.1.1: Percentage Yield

Percentage Yield =
(Actual Yield ÷ Theoretical Yield) x 100

To calculate the percentage yield, follow these steps:
1. Calculate the relative formula masses.

2. Calculate the sum of the relative formula masses using the balanced equation.

3. Calculate theoretical yield using the information from the question.

(Mass of limiting reactant ÷ Sum of M_r for reactant) x Sum of M_r for products

4. Substitute values into percentage yield formula.
Percentage Yield =
(Actual Yield ÷ Theoretical Yield) x 100

Example:

Nitrogen reacts with hydrogen to make ammonia.

$$N_2 + 3H_2 \rightarrow 2NH_3$$

Calculate the percentage yield of ammonia when 24.0g of hydrogen reacts with an excess of nitrogen. The actual yield was 54.0g.

1. Calculate RFM:
   Hydrogen = 2 x 1.0 = 2.0
   Ammonia = 14 + (3 x 1.0) = 17.0

2. Calculate sum of RFM:
   Hydrogen = 2.0 x 3 = 6.0
   Ammonia = 17.0 x 2 = 34.0

3. Calculate Theoretical Yield:
   (24.0 ÷ 6.0) x 34.0 = 136.0

4. Calculate Percentage Yield:
   (54.0 ÷ 136.0) x 100 = 39.7%

Percentage yield varies between 0% and 100%. It may be less than 100% due to:

- Reactants may react in a different way than expected in the air.
- Reaction may not go to completion.
  - Some product may be lost.

C5.1.2: Atom Economy

Atom Economy: Measure of how many atoms in the reactants form the desired product.

A low atom economy means that few atoms in the reactant end up in the desired product.

A high atom economy means that many atoms in the reactant end up in the desired product.

Atom Economy = (Sum of M_r of the desired product ÷ Sum of M_r of all products) x 100

The higher the atom economy of a process, the more sustainable and greener it is.

C5.1.3: Choosing Reaction Pathways

Some of the chemicals we make can have more than one pathway for making them.

Factors considered when selecting a reaction pathway include:
- Yield of the product
- Atom economy
- Rate of the reaction
- By-products made
- Equilibrium position for reversible reactions

By-products are chemicals formed in a reaction in addition to the desired product. Some by-products are useful and can be sold. Other by-products may be toxic or of little use.

C5.1.4: Concentration of a Solution

Common volumes used in chemistry are either cm^3 or dm^3.

- To convert cm^3 to dm^3: DIVIDE by 1000
- To convert dm^3 to cm^3: MULTIPLY by 1000

Concentration can be calculated as g/dm^3 by using the following:

Mass of solute (g) $\div$ Volume of solution (dm^3)

Concentration can also be calculated as mol/dm^3 using the formula:

Amount of solute (mol) $\div$ Volume of solution (dm^3)

To calculate the amount in mol use the formula:

Mass (g) ÷ Molar Mass (g/mol)

Exam hint: Check the units carefully in the question to make sure you have converted as needed.

C5.1.5: Titration

Titration: Method used to determine the concentration of an acid or alkali by using a neutralisation reaction.

It uses a single indicator such as phenolphthalein as it gives a clear end point due to the distinct colour change.

Key indicators used:

Indicator	Colour in acidic solution	Colour in alkaline solution
Litmus	Red	Blue
Phenolphthalein	Colourless	Pink
Methyl Orange	Red	Yellow

Standard solutions with a known accurate concentration are used in titrations.

To make a standard solution of sodium hydroxide:

- Measure 1.00g of sodium hydroxide and dissolve in about 150cm^3 of water in a beaker.
- Add the solution to a 250cm^3 volumetric flask.
- Add water to reach the 250cm^3 mark on the flask.

To carry out a titration:

- Fill the burette with acid.
- Use a volumetric pipette to transfer 25.0cm3 of sodium hydroxide (alkali) to a conical flask.
- Add a few drops of a single indicator to the flask.
- Record the start volume from the burette.
- Gradually add acid from the burette to the flask until it just changes colour.
- Record the end volume from the burette.

Burette

You need to repeat the method until you have concordant titres, within 0.10cm^3 of each other.

Titre: A measured volume of solution added from a burette during a titration to reach the end point.

When considering the accuracy of a titration, you should consider:
- Measuring cylinders can be used to measure the 25cm^3 of solution for the conical flask but these are less accurate than a volumetric pipette.

- Burettes must be clamped vertically for accurate results.

- Always read from the bottom of the meniscus with your eye level with this line.

- Record to 2 decimal places. If the bottom of the meniscus is on a line, the second decimal place is a 0. If the bottom of the meniscus is between two lines, the second decimal place is a 5.

- The flask should be swirled during titrations to mix the contents.

- Add drop by drop as you approach the end point.

C5.1.6: Titration Calculations

After a titration has been carried out we know:
- The two reactants used
- The volume AND concentration of one reactant
- The volume of the other reactant

This information can be used to calculate the unknown concentration using the formula:

Amount in mol = Concentration in mol/dm^3 x Volume in dm^3

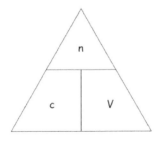

Method 1:

$25.00cm^3$ of $0.100mol/dm^3$ sodium hydroxide was titrated with dilute hydrochloric acid. The mean titre of the acid was $20.00cm^3$. Calculate the concentration of the acid.

$HCl\ (aq) + NaOH\ (aq) \rightarrow NaCl\ (aq) + H_2O\ (l)$

Step 1: Convert cm^3 to dm^3.
Volume of NaOH = $25.00 \div 1000$ = $0.025dm^3$
Volume of HCl = $20.00 \div 1000$ = $0.020dm^3$

Step 2: Calculate the amount of the reactant you have volume and concentration for.
Amount = Concentration x Volume
= 0.100×0.025
= 0.0025 mol

Step 3: Use the balanced equation to work out the amount of the other reactant.

1 mol NaOH reacts with 1 mol HCl

So 0.0025 mol of NaOH will react with 0.0025 mol HCl

Step 4: Use the equation to work out the unknown concentration.

Concentration = Amount ÷ Volume

= 0.0025 ÷ 0.020

= 0.125 mol/dm³

Method 2:

Step 1: Fill in the table with what you know from the question.

	Acid	Alkali
Amount (mol)		
Volume (dm³)	20 ÷ 1000 = 0.020	25 ÷ 1000 = 0.025
Concentration (mol/dm³)		0.100

Step 2: Calculate the missing value for the column where you have only one space.

	Acid	Alkali
Amount (mol)		0.100 ÷ 0.025 = 0.0025
Volume (dm³)	20 ÷ 1000 = 0.020	25 ÷ 1000 = 0.025
Concentration (mol/dm³)		0.100

Step 3: Use the balanced equation to work out the amount in mol for the other chemical.

	Acid	Alkali
Amount (mol)	0.0025	0.100 ÷ 0.025 = 0.0025
Volume (dm³)	20 ÷ 1000 = 0.020	25 ÷ 1000 = 0.025
Concentration (mol/dm³)		0.100

Step 4: Calculate the final empty box.

	Acid	Alkali
Amount (mol)	0.0025	0.100 ÷ 0.025 = 0.0025
Volume (dm^3)	20 ÷ 1000 = 0.020	25 ÷ 1000 = 0.025
Concentration (mol/dm^3)	0.0025 ÷ 0.020 = 0.125	0.100

The key steps to carrying out titration calculations are:

1. Convert volumes to dm^3 (divide by 1000)
2. Calculate the amount of the reactant you know volume and concentration for.
3. Use the balanced equation to work out the amount of the other reactant.
4. Use the equation to work out the unknown concentration.

C5.1.7: Gas Calculations

One mole of any substance in the gas state occupies the same volume at the same temperature and pressure. This is the molar volume.

At room temperature and pressure (RTP), this is $24 \text{dm}^3/\text{mol}$.

To calculate the volume of a gas at RTP, use the following formula:
Volume in dm^3 =
Amount in mol x $24 \text{dm}^3/\text{mol}$

Example question:

2.62g of zinc reacts with excess sulphuric acid.
$Zn(s) + H_2SO_4 (aq) \rightarrow ZnSO_4 (aq) + H_2 (g)$
Calculate the volume of hydrogen produced at RTP.

Step 1: Calculate the amount of limiting reactant.
Zinc molar mass= 65.4
Amount of zinc = 2.62 ÷ 65.4
= 0.040 mol

Step 2: Work out the amount of hydrogen produced using the balanced equation.
1 mole of zinc makes 1 mole of hydrogen.
So, 0.040 mol of zinc will make 0.040 mol of hydrogen.

Step 3: Calculate the volume of hydrogen.
$0.040 \times 24 = 0.96 dm^3$

Check Your Understanding

1. What formula is used to calculate percentage yield?

2. What formula is used to calculate atom economy?

3. Give two reasons why the percentage yield may not be 100%.

4. State four factors to consider when selecting a reaction pathway.

5. What is the formula for calculating concentration?

6. Explain how to use titration to find the concentration of an unknown solution.

7. What is the formula for calculating gas volume?

C5.2.1: Rate of Reaction

Reaction rate: Measure of how quickly reactants are used or products are formed.

Rate of reaction = Amount ÷ Time

Two key ways to measure the volume of gas made in a reaction:

1. Fill a measuring cylinder with water. Turn it upside-down in a tub of water. Place a delivery tube underneath.

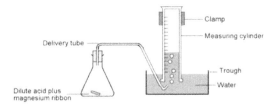

2. Use a gas syringe

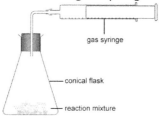

To calculate the rate:

- Calculate the changes in volume and time across the period specified in the question.
  - Calculate the mean gradient.
    Gradient =
    Change in Volume ÷ Change in Time

If you are asked to calculate the rate at a specific point, draw a tangent to the curve.

To do this:
- Put a ruler against the point on the curve you are investigating.
- Adjust the angle of the ruler so it is an equal distance from the curve on each side of the point.
- Draw a line using the ruler.
- Make it a right-angled triangle and use the change in volume and time.

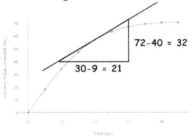

72-40 = 32

30-9 = 21

C5.2.2: Temperature and Reaction Rate & PAG C8

A common way to investigate the rate of reaction and the impact of changing the temperature is with sodium thiosulphate and hydrochloric acid.

1. Place a beaker onto a piece of paper with 10 crosses drawn on it.
2. Add $25cm^3$ of sodium thiosulphate to the beaker.
3. Measure $10cm^3$ of acid in a measuring cylinder.
4. Add the acid to the beaker and start the stop watch.
5. Stop the stop watch when you can no longer see the crosses.

When we increase the temperature, the rate of reaction increases. This is because when the temperature increases, the particles gain kinetic energy and move faster. They will have more frequent successful collisions.

The rate of reaction is inversely proportional to the reaction time. This means 1 ÷ time is directly proportional to the rate.

1 ÷ Reaction Time α Rate of Reaction

C5.2.3: Concentration, Pressure and Reaction Rate

Concentration: Measure of how much solute is dissolved in the solvent.
A more concentrated solution has a greater mass of solute dissolved in the solvent.

When the concentration is increased, the rate of reaction increases. In higher concentrations, the particles are more crowded so they have more frequent collisions.

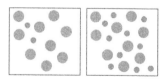

The reaction will stop when the limiting reactant has been used up. You can tell when the reaction stops as the graph plateaus.

The amount of product is proportional to the amount of limiting reactant.

If the pressure increases, the particles become more crowded and so collide more frequently so the rate is faster.

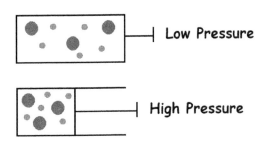

Low Pressure

High Pressure

C5.2.4: Particle Size and Reaction Rate

When a material is broken up into smaller pieces, the surface area increases. A powder has a larger surface area than a single lump of the same mass.

When surface area increases, the rate of reaction increases. As the size of the lump decreases, the surface area to volume ratio increases. This is because there are more exposed particles so there are more frequent collisions.

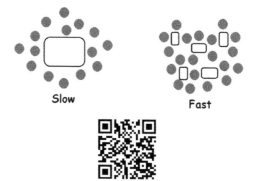

Slow

Fast

C5.2.5: Catalysts and Reaction Rate

A catalyst is a substance that increases the rate of a reaction but is unchanged at the end of the reaction. They are specific to a reaction.

When a catalyst is added, the rate of reaction increases. This is because they provide an alternative reaction pathway with a lower activation energy. This means that a greater proportion of the colliding particles reach the activation energy.

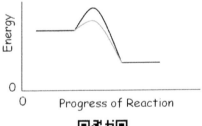

Check Your Understanding

1. Suggest two methods for measuring the volume of a gas made in a chemical reaction.

2. Explain how to calculate the rate of a reaction from a graph.

3. Explain the effect of changes in temperature on the rate of a reaction.

4. Explain the effect of changes in concentration on the rate of a reaction.

5. Explain the effect of changes in pressure on the rate of a reaction.

6. Explain the effect of changes in particle size on the rate of a reaction.

7. Explain the effect of using a catalyst on the rate of a reaction.

C5.3.1: Reversible Reactions

In a reversible reaction, the products can react together to form the original reactants. They have both a forward and backward reaction.
They use the symbol: $\rightleftharpoons$

E.g.

$CuSO_4.5H_2O \rightleftharpoons CuSO_4 + 5H_2O$

Forward reaction:

$CuSO_4.5H_2O \rightarrow CuSO_4 + 5H_2O$

Backward reaction:

$CuSO_4 + 5H_2O \rightarrow CuSO_4.5H_2O$

If a reversible reaction occurs in a closed system (nothing can enter or leave), it reaches a dynamic equilibrium. This means the rate of the forward and backward reactions are equal. The concentrations of all reacting substances remain constant.

C5.3.2: Equilibrium Position

The equilibrium position is a description of the relative amounts of reactants and products in a reaction mixture at equilibrium.

The equilibrium position is on the left when the concentration of reactants is greater than the concentration of products.

The equilibrium position is on the right when the concentration of reactants is less than the concentration of products.

The equilibrium position may change with altered conditions.

Changing Pressure

If you increase the pressure, the equilibrium position moves in the direction of the fewest moles of gas.

$$2SO_2 \text{ (g)} + O_2 \text{ (g)} \rightleftharpoons 2SO_3 \text{ (g)}$$

There are 3 moles of gas on the left and 2 moles of gas on the right. So, increasing the pressure moves the equilibrium position to the right.

Changing Concentration

If you increase the concentration of a substance, the equilibrium position moves in the direction away from that substance.

$$HCl \text{ (aq)} + CaCO_3 \text{ (s)} \rightleftharpoons CaCl_2 \text{ (aq)} + H_2O \text{ (l)} + CO_2 \text{ (g)}$$

If we increase the concentration of hydrochloric acid, the equilibrium position moves to the right.

Changing Temperature

If you increase the temperature of a substance, the equilibrium position moves in the direction of the endothermic change.

$2NO_2$ (g) $\rightleftharpoons$ N_2O_4 (g) (ΔH = -58kJ/mol)

The forward reaction is exothermic due to the – sign.

This means the backward reaction is endothermic.

So, the equilibrium position moves to the left.

Remember:

Pressure: Towards the fewest moles of gas.

Concentration: Away from the substance with increased concentration.

Temperature: Direction of the endothermic reaction (ΔH = +)

C5.3.3: Choosing Reaction Conditions

Methanol is produced by reacting carbon monoxide with hydrogen.

$$CO\ (g) + 2H_2\ (g) \rightleftharpoons CH_3OH\ (g)$$
$$(\Delta H = -91kJ/mol)$$

The equilibrium yield (amount of desired product present at equilibrium) depends upon:
- Pressure
- Temperature
- Concentration of reactants

To increase the amount of methanol made, we need to move the equilibrium position to the right.

Changing the Pressure

Increasing the pressure moves the equilibrium position in the direction of the fewest moles of gas.
As we have 3 moles of gas on the left and 1 on the right, increasing the pressure will increase the yield of methanol.

Pressure is often a compromise due to the equipment cost and safety aspects. High pressures need expensive equipment to compress the gases and reaction vessels capable of withstanding the pressure. It also requires lots of energy to do this. All these factors cost money.

The compromise pressure is high enough to give a reasonable equilibrium yield but not high enough to be expensive or hazardous.

Changing the Temperature

The forward reaction is exothermic (- sign) so the backward reaction is endothermic.

Increasing the temperature moves the equilibrium position to the left so the yield of methanol would decrease.

A compromise is used with temperature in this situation. It needs to be low enough to achieve a reasonable equilibrium yield but not too low to have a very slow rate of reaction.

Check Your Understanding

1. What is the symbol for a reversible reaction?

2. What is meant by the term dynamic equilibrium?

3. Explain what happens to the equilibrium position when the pressure is changed.

4. Explain what happens to the equilibrium position when the temperature is changed.

5. Explain what happens to the equilibrium position when the concentration is changed.

6. Explain why we use a compromise for pressure and temperature for some reactions.

C6
Global
Challenges

C6.1.1: Fertilisers

Essential elements are the elements that plants require for growth. They are:
- Nitrogen
- Phosphorus
- Potassium

Element	Mineral Deficiency Symptoms
Nitrogen	Poor growth, yellow leaves
Phosphorus	Poor root growth, discoloured leaves
Potassium	Poor fruit growth, discoloured leaves

Fertilisers replace the elements used by plants as they grow. The fertiliser must be soluble in water so it dissolves and is absorbed through the roots of the plant.

The minerals absorbed are:

- Nitrogen as nitrate ions, NO_3^-, or ammonium ions, NH_4^+.
- Phosphorus in phosphate ions, PO_4^{3-}.
- Potassium as potassium ions, K^+.

NPK fertilisers provide the three essential elements mentioned to the plants in differing ratios, depending on the fertiliser selected.

Ammonia is a very important chemical when making fertilisers. The Haber process makes ammonia from nitrogen and hydrogen. This is a reversible reaction.

$$N_2 (g) + 3H_2 (g) \rightleftharpoons 2NH_3 (g)$$

The raw materials for the Haber process are air, natural gas and steam.

Nitrogen is made from the fractional distillation of liquefied air.

Hydrogen is made by reacting natural gas with steam.

A range of compounds are made in a fertiliser factory which will be used to create fertilisers for different needs.

These include:
- Ammonium nitrate, NH_4NO_3
- Ammonium sulphate, $(NH_4)_2SO_4$
- Ammonium phosphate, $(NH_4)_3PO_4$
- Potassium nitrate, KNO_3

C6.1.2: Making Fertilisers

Fertilisers can be made by neutralising an acid with an alkali to make the neutral salt.

Acid + Alkali → Salt + Water

E.g.

Potassium hydroxide + Sulphuric Acid →
Potassium Sulphate + Water

To work out the endings for the salt:

Hydrochloric Acid → Chloride
Sulphuric Acid → Sulphate
Nitric Acid → Nitrate
Phosphoric Acid → Phosphate

As making fertilisers requires a titration in the lab, we use a single indicator.

Indicator	Colour in acidic solution	Colour in alkaline solution
Litmus	Red	Blue
Phenolphthalein	Colourless	Pink
Methyl Orange	Red	Yellow

Method:

1. Fill the burette with acid.
2. Use a volumetric pipette to transfer 25cm^3 of alkali to the conical flask.
3. Add a few drops of indicator.
4. Record the start volume.
5. Add the acid, while swirling the flask, until the indicator changes colour.
6. Record the end volume.
7. Repeat until you obtain concordant readings, within 0.10cm^3.
8. Add activated charcoal (this attracts the phenolphthalein).
9. Filter the solution.
10. Evaporate the solution to leave the fertiliser crystals.

When we consider the difference in the processes used when making chemicals in industry, there are two key processes we need to know about.

They are:

1. Batch Process: Used to make speciality chemicals (pharmaceuticals) as they are only needed in small amounts.
2. Continuous Process: Used to make bulk chemicals as they are needed in large amounts.

Factors to consider when comparing:

Feature	Batch	Continuous
Rate of production	Low	High
Relative cost of equipment	Low	High
Number of workers needed	Large	Small
Shut-down periods	Frequent	Rare
Ease of automation	Low	High

C6.1.3: The Haber Process

This is used to make ammonia.

The conditions chosen are:
- 450°C temperature
- 200 atmosphere pressure
- Iron catalyst

This gives a yield of approximately 30%.

Why 450°C?

The forward reaction is exothermic and the backward reaction is endothermic. So, increasing the temperature, moves the equilibrium position to the left which decreases the yield of ammonia.

The lower the temperature, the higher the yield of ammonia BUT the higher the temperature, the faster the rate of reaction. A compromise of 450°C is chosen between rate and yield.

Why 200 atmospheres?

$$N_2 (g) + 3H_2 (g) \rightleftharpoons 2NH_3 (g)$$

If the pressure is increased, the equilibrium position moves to the right and the yield increases as there are fewer moles of gas on the right.

The compromise of 200 atmospheres is used as it gives a high yield without extravagant costs and risks due to high pressure.

Why recycle?

The gases leaving the reaction vessel are cooled. This condenses the ammonia to a liquid which is run off and the unreacted hydrogen and nitrogen are pumped back into the reaction vessel to reduce waste.

C6.1.4: The Contact Process

The Contact process is used to make sulphuric acid.

It needs three raw materials:
- Sulphur
- Air
- Water

There are three stages to the process.

Stage 1

Sulphur burns in air to produce sulphur dioxide.

$$S(s) + O_2(g) \rightarrow SO_2(g) \quad (\Delta H = -297 kJ/mol)$$

Stage 2

Sulphur dioxide and oxygen react to produce sulphur trioxide (SO_3).

$$2SO_2(g) + O_2(g) \rightleftharpoons 2SO_3(g)$$
$$(\Delta H = -144 kJ/mol)$$

Conditions chosen for stage 2 are:
- 2 atmospheres
- 450°C
- Vanadium oxide catalyst

This produces a 96% yield.

As the equilibrium position is far to the right already, high pressures are not needed. The 2 atmospheres is enough to move the gases through the converter.

The forward reaction is exothermic so the backward reaction is endothermic. A high equilibrium yield is favoured by low temperatures. The temperature used is a compromise between yield and reaction rate. Vanadium oxide only works above 380°C.

Stage 3

Sulphur trioxide is converted to sulphuric acid through the addition of water.
$$H_2O \text{ (l)} + SO_3 \text{ (g)} \rightarrow H_2SO_4 \text{ (aq)}$$

The stage 3 reaction is very exothermic. If it was carried out as one step, it would create a dangerous acidic mist. Stage 3 is split into two processes to make it safer:

1. Sulphur trioxide is passed through concentrated sulphuric acid to make oleum, $H_2S_2O_7$.
$$H_2SO_4 \text{ (l)} + SO_3 \text{ (g)} \rightarrow H_2S_2O_7 \text{ (l)}$$

2. Oleum is added to water to make a large volume of concentrated sulphuric acid.
$$H_2S_2O_7 \text{ (l)} + H_2O \text{ (l)} \rightarrow 2H_2SO_4 \text{ (aq)}$$

C6.1.5: Making Ethanol

Ethanol can be made from either renewable or non-renewable raw materials.

Renewable

Renewable raw materials can be replaced as they are used so they will not run out.

Ethanol is made in a fermentation reaction. Yeast contain enzymes that convert glucose into carbon dioxide and ethanol. The glucose comes from plants.

Glucose → Carbon Dioxide + Ethanol
$$C_6H_{12}O_6 \text{ (aq)} \rightarrow 2CO_2 \text{ (g)} + 2C_2H_5OH \text{ (aq)}$$

If the temperature is too low, the yeast cells become inactive. If too high, the enzymes become denatured (above 50°C). Fermentation is usually carried out at 35°C at normal atmospheric pressure.

Non-Renewable

Non-renewable raw materials are used faster than they can be replaced so they will eventually run out. Ethene comes from crude oil.

Ethene can be hydrated to make ethanol.

Ethene + Water (Steam) $\rightleftharpoons$ Ethanol

C_2H_4 (g) + H_2O (g) $\rightleftharpoons$ C_2H_5OH (g)

(-45kJ/mol)

This experiment requires:
- 300°C
- 60 atmospheres pressure
- Phosphoric acid catalyst

When deciding which process to use to make ethanol, there are a number of factors to consider:

Feature	Fermentation	Hydration
Raw material cost	Low	High
Conditions	Moderate temperature, normal pressure	High temperature and pressure
Energy Needs	Low	High
Rate of Reaction	Low	High
% Yield	Low (15%)	High (95%)
Purity of Product	Low (needs filtering and fractional distillation)	High (No by-products)

C6.1.6: Extracting Metals

An ore is a rock or mineral that contains enough metal to make it economical to extract.

Important ores:
- Malachite contains copper carbonate
- Bauxite contains aluminium oxide
- Haematite contains iron (III) oxide

Ores are extracted by mining and then are processed to separate the metal. The method used to extract the metal from its ore depends on its position in the reactivity series.

Method 1: Electrolysis - Expensive but can extract all metals

Method 2: Heating with carbon or carbon monoxide - Cheaper but only works with metals less reactive than carbon

Extracting Copper

There are two stages:
1) Copper (II) sulphide is roasted in air:

Copper (II) Sulphide + Oxygen →
Copper (II) Oxide + Sulphur Dioxide

$$2CuS (s) + 3O_2 (g) → 2CuO (s) + 2SO_2 (g)$$

2) The copper (II) oxide is heated with carbon:

Copper (II) Oxide + Carbon →
Copper + Carbon Dioxide

$$2CuO (s) + C (s) → 2Cu (s) + CO_2 (g)$$

It is a redox reaction and carbon is the reducing agent.

Copper (II) oxide can also be reduced to copper by heating it with methane or with hydrogen.

C6.1.7: Extracting Iron

Iron is extracted from its ore using a blast furnace.

Raw materials are:
- Iron ore (haematite)
- Coke
- Limestone

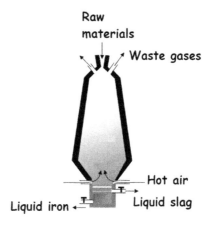

Stage 1:
Coke burns in hot air making carbon dioxide:

$$C \text{ (s)} + O_2 \text{ (g)} \rightarrow CO_2 \text{ (g)}$$

Stage 2:
Coke reduces the carbon dioxide making carbon monoxide:

$$C \text{ (s)} + CO_2 \text{ (g)} \rightarrow 2CO \text{ (g)}$$

Stage 3:
Carbon monoxide reduces Iron (III) Oxide to iron at around 1500°C:

$$3CO \text{ (g)} + Fe_2O_3 \text{ (s)} \rightarrow 3CO_2 \text{ (g)} + 2Fe \text{ (l)}$$

The liquid iron formed at this point has impurities in it. These need to be removed to avoid the properties of the iron being altered.

Limestone is used to remove the impurities in two stages.

Stage 1:
Calcium carbonate decomposes in high temperatures:
$$CaCO_3 \text{ (s)} \rightarrow CaO \text{ (s)} + CO_2 \text{ (g)}$$

Stage 2:
Calcium oxide reacts with silica, SiO_2, to form calcium silicate, $CaSiO_3$:
$$CaO \text{ (s)} + SiO_2 \text{ (g)} \rightarrow CaSiO_3 \text{ (l)}$$

This forms the slag (molten calcium silicate. The slag is less dense than the iron so can be run off separately.

C6.1.8: Extracting Aluminium

Aluminium ore is called bauxite. Aluminium is usually found as aluminium oxide, Al_2O_3.

Aluminium has to be extracted using electrolysis due to aluminium being more reactive than carbon.

Aluminium oxide has a melting point of 2072°C. This means it would be expensive to heat it to melting.

Aluminium oxide is dissolved in molten cryolite which allows electrolysis to happen at about 950°C.

The electrolysis cell is steel lined with graphite. The graphite acts as the cathode. Graphite blocks act as the anodes.

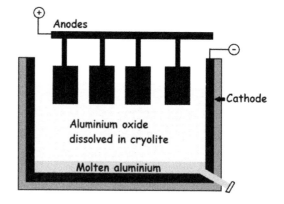

Oxygen is produced at the anode where it reacts with the graphite to make carbon dioxide. Aluminium is produced at the cathode.

At the cathode: $Al^{3+} + 3e^- \rightarrow Al$
At the anode: $2O^{2-} \rightarrow O_2 + 4e^-$

C6.1.9: Biological Metal Extraction

Abandoned mines often flood which leads to the oxidation of metal sulphides to sulphuric acid. The acid then reacts with metal ores creating soluble metal compounds which are carried in the water as it drains from the mine.

Bioleaching

Bacteria oxidise iron (II) and sulphide ions. Sulphuric acid forms when oxygen and water are present. Sulphuric acid breaks down copper sulphide ores to release copper (II) ions.

Advantages:
- Low-grade ores can be used
- Cheaper than traditional methods
- Bacteria occur naturally
- Does not release sulphur dioxide into the atmosphere.

Disadvantages:
- Slow
- Toxic substances may be produced.

Phytoextraction

Some plants are good at absorbing certain metal ions which then accumulate in their roots, shoots and leaves. These plants are used in phytoextraction.

The crop is grown on soil containing low-grade ore or mine waste. A complexing agent is added to the soil to improve absorption of the metal ions. The plants are then harvested and burnt to produce ash with a high metal concentration. The metal is extracted from the ash as if it were a high-grade ore.

Advantages:
- Cheaper than traditional methods
- Less waste
- Smaller energy transfers
- Close to carbon-neutral

Disadvantages:
- Slow
- Crops may need replanting and harvesting for years before all the metal is removed from the soil

C6.1.10: Alloys

An alloy is a mixture of two or more elements where at least one is a metal.

Alloy	Main metal(s)	Uses
Steel	Iron	Buildings, cars
Solder	Tin and copper	Joining wires and pipes
Brass	Copper and zinc	Musical instruments, coins
Bronze	Copper and tin	Bells, ship propellers
Duralumin	Aluminium and copper	Aircraft parts

When considering why certain alloys are used for a specific job, you need to consider the properties.

Solder melts at 227°C which means that it won't damage electrical components as it joins them. It also flows into gaps to fill them before solidifying. It conducts electricity.

In pure copper, the atoms slide over each other easily. In brass, the zinc and copper atoms are different sizes so it makes it more difficult for the copper atoms to slide over each other.

Brass is:
- A good conductor of electricity
- Strong
- Resists corrosion

Bronze is corrosion resistant and is stronger and harder than copper alone. Used in bells and propellers.

C6.1.11: Corrosion

Corrosion is the reaction of a metal with substances in its surroundings.

Silver does not react easily with oxygen. If hydrogen sulphide, H_2S, is present, it reacts with silver when oxygen and water are also present to make silver sulphide, Ag_2S. This makes the silver object appear tarnished.

The only metals that do not corrode the very unreactive ones. E.g. gold, platinum.

Rust is hydrated iron (III) oxide. This means we can only use the term rusting when we are talking about iron. Any other metals corrode.

Rusting is a redox reaction.
Iron + Oxygen + Water →
Hydrated Iron (III) Oxide

The hydrated iron (III) oxide flakes off the surface of the metal easily. This reveals fresh iron and so the process continues.

To carry out an investigation into rusting, we use steel nails placed in test tubes under different conditions:

1. Anhydrous calcium chloride to remove the water from the air. This one will not rust.

2. Boiled water to remove the oxygen. This one will not rust.

3. Air and water. This nail will rust.

C6.1.12: Reducing Corrosion

There are several methods we can use to reduce corrosion of metals. Many of them rely on preventing oxygen and water reaching the surface of the metal. They include:

- Painting
- Coating with oil, grease or plastic
- Plating with zinc
- Plating with tin

Another technique is sacrificial protection. This is where a more reactive metal is placed in contact with the less reactive metal we wish to protect.

During rusting:
$$Fe \rightarrow Fe^{3+} + 3e^-$$
The more reactive the metal, the more easily it loses electrons so they are more readily oxidised.

By attaching a more reactive metal to the less reactive one, we ensure the more reactive metal will corrode first.

The next technique is metal plating. This is where we use another metal to coat the one that needs protecting. It prevents oxygen and water reaching the metal underneath.

If we dip the metal into molten zinc, we have galvanised the metal.

The final technique is tin plating where we electroplate the steel can with tin. Food cans have tin plating inside them. As tin is less reactive than iron, any damage to the coating leads to faster corrosion.

C6.1.13: Different Materials

There are a range of different materials available in the world for us to use. We need to select the right material for the right job.

Ceramics are hard, non-metallic materials. They contain metals and non-metals which combine to form giant ionic lattices or giant covalent structures. Examples of ceramic materials are brick, china, glass and porcelain.

Typical ceramic properties:
- Poor conductors of heat and electricity
  - High melting points
    - Hard
    - Brittle

The compounds in ceramics are mostly oxides and so they are unreactive.

Making Ceramics

Brick – Heat clay to very high temperatures which makes tiny crystals form that are joined together by glass.
China and Porcelain – Heat clay to high temperatures as for brick but then coat it with a glaze and reheat. This forms a waterproof, hard and smooth surface.
Glass – Melt sand and cool so it solidifies to form a giant irregular structure without crystals.

The most common type of question here will be based around selecting a material from a table of information for a particular use. Not all columns on the table will be related to that use so think about what is related and include those as your justification.

C6.1.14: Composite Materials

Composite materials are made from two or more materials with different properties being combined together. The properties of the composite material are different from those of the materials it contains.

E.g. Polycotton is a composite material made from cotton and polyester.

Fibreglass is made when glass fibres are embedded in a resin. This creates a material which is strong and hard but lightweight making it useful in boats.

Carbon fibre is used in sports equipment, racing cars and aircraft parts. It consists of carbon fibres embedded in a resin.

Concrete is made from aggregate, sand and cement. The ingredients are bound together when water is added as it triggers a chemical reaction.

Concrete is useful as a foundation for buildings as it has a high compressive strength. It is not as useful for beams as it has a low tensile strength so may crack when heavy loads are placed on them. To solve this problem steel rods are embedded within the concrete to give it higher tensile strength.

C6.1.15: Choosing Materials

When we consider what material to use to construct an object, we need to consider the properties and how they relate to the use.

E.g.

A cup to hold hot drinks would need to have a high melting point, a high tensile strength and not be too expensive. The ability to conduct electricity is irrelevant as the ability to hold a hot drink is unaffected by if it conducts electricity or not.

> Exam hint: Only talk about the relevant properties in your answer. Some questions will include columns that are not relevant.

Another consideration when selecting materials comes from the life-cycle assessment (LCA). This is a cradle to grave analysis of the impact of making, using and disposing of a product.

Life cycle assessments should include data about:
- Lifespan of the product
- Environmental impact
- Sustainability
- Recycling of any product parts
- Disposal techniques including ease of decomposition

From the LCA we can identify stages that could be improved or where alternative materials could be used to do the same job.

C6.1.16: Recycling Materials

Recycling is an important part of our modern lives. Any of the rubbish we generate that isn't recycled will end up in landfills.

Recycling is important as it:
- Conserves raw materials and energy resources
- Reduces the release of harmful substances into the environment
- Reduces waste

When deciding if a material should be recycled, there are several factors to consider:
- Ease of collection and sorting
- Amount and type of by-products released by recycling
- Amount of energy involved at each stage
- Cost of recycling compared to landfill or incineration

The method used to recycle a material will vary depending on what the material is. All materials are collected and sorted. Then:

- Metals are melted and poured into moulds to produce ingots.
- Paper is mixed with water, cleaned, rolled and heated to make new paper.
- Glass is melted and moulded into new objects.
- Polymers are melted and moulded into new objects.

Check Your Understanding

1. Explain the differences between batch and continuous process.

2. Explain how the Haber process works.

3. Explain the Contact process.

4. Compare the two methods for making ethanol.

5. Describe how to extract iron from its ore.

6. Describe how to extract aluminium.

7. Explain the techniques for biological metal extraction.

8. Describe how materials are chosen for a job.

C6.2.1: Alkanes

Hydrocarbons are compounds made from hydrogen and oxygen only.

Alkanes are hydrocarbons. They form a homologous series as they have the following features in common:
- Same general formula: C_nH_{2n+2}
- They are saturated (only single bonds between the atoms)

Alkane names are made by:
- First part is the number of carbons
- Ending is -ane.

When drawing the displayed formula remember that hydrogen can only make 1 covalent bond and carbon will make 4 covalent bonds.

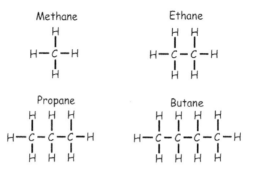

Methane

Ethane

Propane

Butane

Alkane Reactions

The two types of combustion reaction:

1. Complete combustion – Leads to the complete oxidation of the hydrocarbon into carbon dioxide and water.

Hydrocarbon + Oxygen →
Carbon Dioxide + Water

2. Incomplete combustion – Occurs when there is insufficient oxygen to form carbon, carbon monoxide and water.

Hydrocarbon + Oxygen →
Carbon + Carbon Monoxide + Water

C6.2.2: Alkenes

Alkenes are hydrocarbons that form a homologous series. They are unsaturated as they contain a double carbon-carbon bond.

General Formula: C_nH_{2n}

Their name ends in –ene.

Their functional group is C=C.

Functional groups are atoms, groups of atoms or types of bond in a molecule that are responsible for the characteristic reactions of the substance.

Ethene

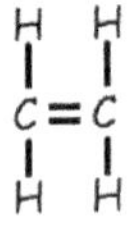

Propene

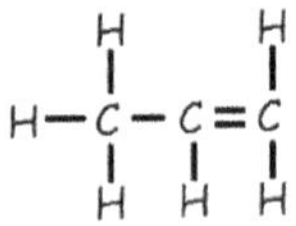

Butene

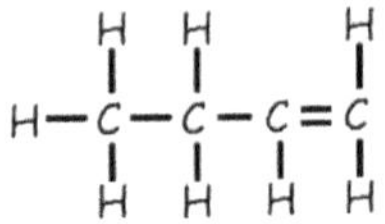

Pentene

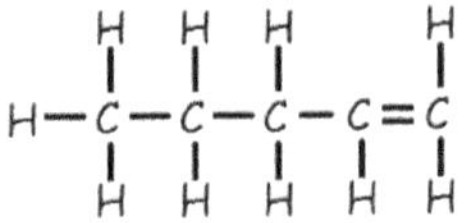

Alkene Reactions

Alkenes undergo combustion reactions with the same products as alkanes.

Alkenes also undergo addition reactions where atoms or groups of atoms combine with a molecule to form a larger molecule with no other product.

We can test a hydrocarbon to identify if it is an alkane or alkene by adding bromine water. If an alkene is present, an addition reaction occurs and we see a colour change from orange-brown to colourless.

$$C_2H_4 + Br_2 \rightarrow C_2H_4Br_2$$

Alkenes can also undergo an addition reaction with hydrogen to produce alkanes. This requires the presence of a nickel catalyst.

C6.2.3: Alcohols

Alcohols form a homologous series.
General formula: $C_nH_{2n+1}OH$
Their names all end in –ol.
Functional group: hydroxyl –OH.

Methanol

$$H-\overset{\displaystyle H}{\underset{\displaystyle H}{C}}-O-H$$

Ethanol

$$H-\overset{\displaystyle H}{\underset{\displaystyle H}{C}}-\overset{\displaystyle H}{\underset{\displaystyle H}{C}}-O-H$$

Propanol

$$H-\overset{\displaystyle H}{\underset{\displaystyle H}{C}}-\overset{\displaystyle H}{\underset{\displaystyle H}{C}}-\overset{\displaystyle H}{\underset{\displaystyle H}{C}}-O-H$$

Butanol

$$H-\overset{\displaystyle H}{\underset{\displaystyle H}{C}}-\overset{\displaystyle H}{\underset{\displaystyle H}{C}}-\overset{\displaystyle H}{\underset{\displaystyle H}{C}}-\overset{\displaystyle H}{\underset{\displaystyle H}{C}}-O-H$$

Alcohol Reactions

Alcohols burn in oxygen to produce carbon dioxide and water when complete combustion occurs. If it is incomplete combustion, then water vapour, carbon monoxide and carbon are produced.
Alcohols can be oxidised to form carboxylic acids.

C6.2.4: Carboxylic Acids

The carboxylic acids form a homologous series.

General formula: $C_nH_{2n+1}COOH$
Their names all end in –anoic acid.
They contain the carboxyl functional group
–COOH.

> Exam hint: Remember that one of the carbon atoms is in the functional group.

Methanoic Acid

Ethanoic Acid

Propanoic Acid

Butanoic Acid

Carboxylic acids form when alcohols react with oxidising agents such as potassium manganate (VII). E.g.

Mix ethanol, potassium manganate (VII) and dilute sulphuric acid and warm it. The purple manganate (VII) ions are reduced to pink manganese (II) ions when the ethanol is oxidised to make ethanoic acid.

Carboxylic acids are weak acids. This means they will react with:
- Metals to produce a salt and hydrogen.
- Alkalis and bases to produce a salt and water.
- Carbonates to produce a salt, water and carbon dioxide.

The salts made from carboxylic acids all have the ending –oate.

C6.2.5: Alkanes from Crude Oil

Crude oil is a fossil fuel. It was formed from the remains of living things that lived in the sea millions of years ago. They became buried deep in the seabed after they died and eventually turned into crude oil.

Crude oil is a non-renewable resource as it is being used up faster than it is made.

Two other fossil fuels are natural gas and coal. All fossil fuels are finite resources. This means they will run out because they are being used up faster than they are being made.

Crude oil is a mixture of many different hydrocarbons. A hydrocarbon is a compound made of hydrogen and carbon only.

The hydrocarbons in crude oil are separated by fractional distillation:

- Hydrocarbons have different boiling points.
- The more carbon atoms, the longer the molecule so the stronger the intermolecular force and the higher the boiling point.
- The fractionating column has a temperature gradient and is hottest at the bottom.
- As vapours rise, they will condense and run off to be collected.
- Each fraction contains many substances with similar boiling points.

Hydrocarbons with the highest boiling point leave at the bottom of the column. Those with the lowest boiling point leave at the top of the column as a gas.

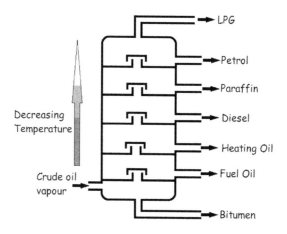

Atoms in the hydrocarbon molecules are joined to each other by covalent bonds. Covalent bonds are stronger than intermolecular forces. So, when crude oil is boiled, the intermolecular forces are overcome which makes the molecules separate to form a vapour.

C6.2.6: Cracking

A key problem with hydrocarbons is that through fractional distillation we end up with a surplus (too much) of the large fractions and a deficit (too little) of smaller fractions. The process of cracking helps match supply to demand for the fractions.

Cracking is used to convert large alkane molecules into smaller, more useful hydrocarbon molecules (alkane and alkene). To carry out cracking we need:
- Catalyst (alumina or silica)
- High temperature (600-700°C)

E.g. Octane → Hexane + Ethene
$$C_8H_{18} \rightarrow C_6H_{14} + C_2H_4$$

C6.2.7: Addition Polymers

Plastics are polymers. A polymer is made from many alkene monomer molecules being joined together.

Addition polymers undergo an addition reaction when they join together. They can do this because of the double bond (C=C). To make the polymer you will need a high pressure and a catalyst.

Naming
If given the monomer and asked to name the polymer – copy the monomer name and then put the word 'poly' in front.
E.g. Monomer = ethane
Polymer = polyethene

If you are given the name of the polymer and asked to give the name of the monomer – copy the polymer name without the poly.

Drawing Displayed Formulae

If you are given the monomer's displayed formula, copy it into the answer space BUT change the double bond for a single bond. Then put square brackets around the formula. Place bonds sticking out the side from the carbons in the middle. Put the letter 'n' in the bottom right.

$$
\begin{array}{cc}
\text{F} & \text{F} \\
| & | \\
\text{C} = \text{C} \\
| & | \\
\text{F} & \text{F}
\end{array}
\qquad
\left[
\begin{array}{cc}
\text{F} & \text{F} \\
| & | \\
\text{C} - \text{C} \\
| & | \\
\text{F} & \text{F}
\end{array}
\right]_n
$$

Monomer   Polymer

If you are given the polymer, then copy the displayed formula without the 'n' or brackets. Change the single bond between the C atoms to a double bond and do not draw the bonds sticking out the side.

C6.2.8: Biological Polymers

DNA is a biological polymer made of monomers called nucleotides. Each nucleotide consists of:
- Phosphate group
- Deoxyribose sugar
- Base

The block diagram of the nucleotide is:

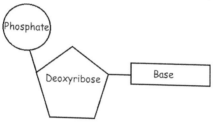

The four bases are:
- Adenine (A)
- Thymine (T)
- Cytosine (C)
- Guanine (G)

Hydrogen bonds form between the bases of the two strands of DNA to hold the double helix shape together.

Proteins are polymers made from monomers called amino acids. There are 20 amino acids that occur naturally in our body. Each has a reactive functional group at the end that enables them to join end to end.

Carbohydrates are made from compounds of carbon, hydrogen and oxygen. The monomers are simple sugars which can be joined to make complex carbohydrates. E.g. Glucose monomers are joined together to make starch.

C6.2.9: Condensation Polymers

In a condensation reaction, two molecules react together to form one larger molecule and one smaller molecule, often water.

Carboxylic Acid + Alcohol → Ester + Water

Condensation polymers are formed by condensation reactions. They do not require a catalyst and occur at room temperature and pressure.

The monomers for condensation polymers need two functional groups.
E.g. Proteins are made from amino acids which have two functional groups:
- Amino group, $-NH_2$
- Carboxyl group, $-COOH$

The monomers are joined by an amide group, $-CONH-$

Polyester is an artificial condensation polymer. It is made from:

- Carboxylic acid with 2 carboxyl groups.
  - Alcohol with two hydroxyl groups.

They form many ester groups when formed, hence their name. Uses include clothing and drinks bottles (PET).

Polyamide is an artificial condensation polymer. It is made from:

- Carboxylic acid with 2 carboxyl groups.
  - Amine with two amino groups.

They form many amide groups when formed, hence their name.
E.g. Nylon which is used in carpets and clothing.

C6.2.10: Producing Electricity Using Chemistry

Chemical cells have an exothermic reaction within the cell that develops a potential difference between the two ends.
When the cell is connected into a circuit, a current flows through the cell and the circuit components.

A fuel cell produces electricity through a chemical reaction between a fuel and oxygen without combustion occurring.

Hydrogen reacts with oxygen in an exothermic reaction to produce water vapour. Hydrogen-oxygen fuel cells use this reaction but it is separated into two reactions, one on each side of the cell.

1) Hydrogen molecules lose electrons to become hydrogen ions.
$$2H_2 \text{ (g)} \rightarrow 4H^+ \text{ (aq)} + 4e^-$$

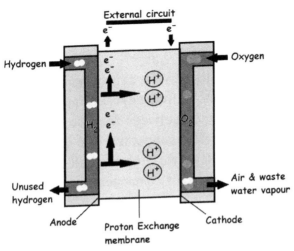

Hydrogen ions pass through the proton exchange membrane to the other side of the fuel cell. The electrons travel through an external circuit to the other side of the fuel cell.

2) Hydrogen ions combine with oxygen and electrons to make water vapour.

$$4H^+ (aq) + O_2 (g) + 4e^- \rightarrow 2H_2O (g)$$

Advantages:
- Lightweight
- Compact
- No moving parts
- No combustion
- No carbon dioxide emissions
- Only waste product is water
- Plenty of hydrogen – decomposed from water

Disadvantages:
- Currently most hydrogen is made through the use of fossil fuels
- Poisonous catalysts in fuels cells that have to be safely disposed of at the end of the fuel cell life

Check Your Understanding

1. What is the general formula for an alkane?

2. Explain the difference between alkanes and alkenes.

3. What is the functional group in alcohols?

4. What is the general formula for carboxylic acids?

5. Explain fractional distillation.

6. Explain the process of cracking and its importance.

7. Name a biological polymer.

8. Explain how a hydrogen-oxygen fuel cell works.

C6.3.1: Forming the Atmosphere

The Earth is 4.54 billion years old.
In the early stages of the planet's development, there was a lot of volcanic activity. This released large volumes of water vapour and carbon dioxide.

As the Earth cooled, the water vapour condensed to form oceans. This left an atmosphere that comprised mainly of carbon dioxide with small amounts of ammonia and methane.

After the appearance of algae and plants, photosynthesis occurred which reduced the amount of carbon dioxide in the atmosphere.
Carbon Dioxide + Water →
Glucose + Oxygen

The oxygen made in the oceans, reacted with the metal to make metal oxides.

After most of the metal had been oxidised, the free oxygen began to accumulate in the atmosphere.

Our current atmosphere has:
78% Nitrogen
21% Oxygen
0.9% Argon
0.04% Carbon Dioxide

C6.3.2: Pollution and the Atmosphere

Pollutants: Substances released into the environment that may harm living things.

Carbon monoxide is made during the incomplete combustion of fuels that contain carbon. It happens when fuels are burnt in a poor supply of oxygen and in vehicle engines.

Carbon monoxide gas is colourless, odourless and tasteless. It binds to the haemoglobin in red blood cells. This reduces the ability of the red blood cells to carry oxygen.

Carbon monoxide poisoning causes:
- Drowsiness
- Difficulty breathing
- Nausea
- Headache
- Death

Particulates are small particles produced during incomplete combustion or industrial processes. The smallest particulates settle deep in the lungs when breathed in leading to bronchitis, breathing problems and increases the chance of heart disease.

Nitrogen and oxygen do not normally react together as nitrogen has a triple bond between its atoms which requires high temperatures to break. Under the high temperatures in vehicle engines, nitrogen does react with oxygen making nitrogen monoxide, NO. NO is oxidised in air to make nitrogen dioxide, NO_2. These oxides of nitrogen are called NO_x.

Nitrogen dioxide dissolves in the water vapour of clouds forming an acidic solution that falls as acid rain.

Acid rain:
- Erodes stonework
- Corrodes metal
- Kills trees
- Kills living things in lakes and rivers.

When fossil fuels are burnt, sulphur dioxide is made as they contain small amounts of sulphur compounds as impurities.
Sulphur dioxide also causes acid rain.
It can also cause breathing difficulties.

C6.3.3: Climate Change

The greenhouse gases are:
- Carbon Dioxide
- Methane
- Water vapour

Radiation from the Sun reaches the Earth's surface where it is absorbed and warms it. The Earth emits infrared radiation. Some goes into space but some is absorbed by greenhouse gases. They then emit infrared radiation in all directions warming the Earth. The more greenhouse gas molecules, the greater the effect.

Anthropogenic (human) activities can increase the amount of greenhouse gases in the atmosphere. This can lead to an enhanced greenhouse effect leading to an increase in the mean surface temperature of the Earth.

Combustion of fossil fuels increase carbon dioxide levels.

Paddy fields; cattle; landfills and natural gas use increase methane levels.

Impacts:
- Ice caps melting and flooding
- Drought
- Extreme weather events

Steps to reduce greenhouse emissions:
- Reduce consumption of fossil fuels
- Use carbon capture techniques to stop carbon dioxide escaping in fuel use.

We can protect against the effects by using flood barriers and designing buildings to withstand extreme weather.

C6.3.4: Water for Drinking

Tap water has originally come from:
- Lakes
- Reservoirs
- Aquifers
- Rivers
- Waste water

Possible contaminants:
- Insoluble materials (leaves, soil)
- Soluble substances (salts; pollutants)
- Microorganisms

The process can be summarised as:
- Filtration using a metal screen –
Removes the large objects like twigs

- Sedimentation in the settlement tank –
Soil and sand sinks to the bottom

- Aluminium sulphate and lime are added – Causes clumping of small particles so they sink to the bottom

- Filtration using fine sand – Removes the small objects like grit

- Chlorination – Kills bacteria

- pH check and correction

- Storage in tanks and reservoirs

Seawater contains high concentrations of dissolved salts. Desalination is the process that removes these salts to make the water potable. Small scale desalination uses reverse osmosis using ultrafilters to filter out the salts. Large scale desalination uses simple distillation.

Check Your Understanding

1. Describe how the atmosphere has changed over the history of the Earth.

2. What is the composition of the atmosphere today?

3. Name two pollutants and explain their impact.

4. Explain the greenhouse effect.

5. List two greenhouse gases.

6. List three problems of the greenhouse effect.

7. Describe how we make potable (drinking) water.

About Wright Science

Wright Science is a YouTube channel created by Vicki Wright, a secondary science teacher in England.

I started Wright Science as a resource for my own classes to have extra help outside of school time. It started with a single recap video for each exam back in 2013 and then just grew. These days there are videos for every lesson on both the separate science courses and combined science courses which are used by a number of students across the country and world!

I hope that you find this book useful and welcome your comments.

Good luck in your exams!

Printed in Great Britain
by Amazon

79720492R00082